A POCKETFUL OF
PYTHON

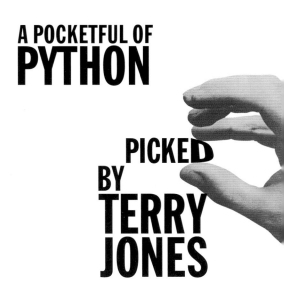

PICKED
BY
TERRY
JONES

WITH A PREFACE BY TERRY GILLIAM

methuen

WRITTEN AND CONCEIVED BY GRAHAM CHAPMAN, JOHN CLEESE TERRY GILLIAM, ERIC IDLE TERRY JONES AND MICHAEL PALIN

DESIGN BY KATY HEPBURN AND ALUN EVANS

Photography by Jim Keary
Rat pie by Margaret
Co-ordinating editor for the *Pocketful of Python* series: Geoffrey Strachan

The texts included in this volume are taken from the TV scripts for *Monty Python's Flying Circus*, published by Methuen in 1989 as *Monty Python's Flying Circus: Just the Words*; the film screenplays for *Monty Python and the Holy Grail, The Life of Brian* and *The Meaning of Life*, published by Methuen in 1977, 1979, and 1983; *Monty Python's Big Red Book* (Methuen 1971); *The Brand New Monty Python Bok*, published in paperback as *The Brand New Monty Python Papperbok* (Methuen 1973 and 1974); and the German Television Special *Monty Python's Fliegender Zirkus* (1972).

Published by Methuen 1999
1 3 5 7 9 10 8 6 4 2

First published in Great Britain by
Methuen Publishing Limited 215 Vauxhall Bridge Road, London SW1V 1EJ

Peribo Pty Ltd, 58 Beaumont Road, Mount Kuring-Gai
NSW 2080, Australia ACN 002 273 761
(for Australia and New Zealand)

Methuen Publishing Limited Reg. No 3543167
A CIP catalogue record for this title is available from the British Library

ISBN 0 413 73290 8
Printed and bound in Great Britain by Butler and Tanner Ltd, Frome, Somerset

A PREFACE BY THE
OTHER TERRY

Terry Jones is a sack of stories. A great wobbly sack like the one Father Christmas bundles around on his back, but full of wondrous smelly things, plump pictures, foolish, outrageous and naughty creatures, tumescent vicars.

He's always seemed round to me. When I first met Terry he wasn't physically round as he has become (beware the Ides of Creosote) - but 'round' always seemed to describe him. His insatiable appetite for life and food and wine and sex and passionately held beliefs has always seemed to demand a big round container in which to stockpile them.

Luckily for Terry, this container has many interesting orifices to provide entrance and egress for life's little pleasures - and the massive amounts of material that interest him. Terry has always shared them with us - not the orifices, but the material.

Sometimes the stuff coming out is just hot air and noxious gasses but more often it is stories and tales, histories and myths, dreams and fabulous worlds, serious and important ideas. These marvels have all managed to find an exit point before Terry's internal pressure gauge reached danger levels.

Thank God! I would hesitate to imagine the mess if they hadn't.

TG May 1999

INTRODUCTION

What I remember most about the making of Monty Python is the curry. We would sit together and plan the shows over a *rhogan josh* and a bit of *dal*, and then go our separate ways to try out the *raita*, the *sag aloo* and the *onion bhajees*, before getting back together again for a *lamb masala*, *prawn biryani*, *meat dopiaza* and a *chicken chat*. Sometimes the curries lasted until the early hours of the morning. We'd all be there - Graham, John, Mike, Terry G and Eric, battling to put away the last of the *patia* or the final bit of *korma*, knowing that by the morning the BBC would expect us to have a complete vegetarian *thali* assembled or at the least a working outline of a decent *bhuna gosht* or a cracking *vindaloo* with plenty of *shaslick* and *oree bhaji* on the side! My goodness, how we fought the BBC Light Entertainment bosses over our right to include *kaboli mutter* and *aloo zeera* as genuine recipes, and how we battled over the *mutter paneer* and the *chana mossala* that they claimed would never be tolerated by our customers in the more provincial cities.

But we showed 'em. We proved that a decent standard of vegetable curry is as acceptable to the majority of people as a *chicken jalfriizi* or a *king prawn dansak*.

So when I was asked to put together this selection of my favourite texts from the Monty Python books, shows and films, I naturally went for the one that expressed the true essence of Python - the curries. I deliberately avoided any sketches or extracts that did not include at least one or more of the following words: "tandoori", "balti", "Ceylon", "pasanda", "paratha", "bindi" or "brinjal bhaji".

I apologize if readers feel this has constrained my choice unnecessarily, but I believe it is better to include less, but more essentially Pythonic, material than just anything that made me laugh.

So "peshwari nan" to you all and I hope you enjoy this Punjabi feast of fun.

TJ April 1999

THE **FRENCH** TAUNT **KING** ARTHUR

You don't frighten us, English pig-dog. Go and boil your bottom, son of a silly person. I blow my nose on you so-called Arthur King, you and your silly English k....niggetsI don't want to talk to you no more, you empty- headed animal food trough wiper. I fart in your general direction. Your mother was a hamster and your father smelled of elderberries.

THE TRUTH ABOUT
PROTESTANTS

MR BLACKITT: Look at them, bloody Catholics. Filling the bloody world up with bloody people they can't afford to bloody feed.

MRS BLACKITT: What are we dear?

MR BLACKITT: Protestants, and fiercely proud of it....

MRS BLACKITT: Why do they have so many children....?

MR BLACKITT: Because every time they have sexual intercourse they have to have a baby.

MRS BLACKITT: But it's the same with us, Harry.

MR BLACKITT: What d'you mean...?

MRS BLACKITT: Well I mean we've got two children and we've had sexual intercourse twice.

MR BLACKITT: That's not the point.... We could have it any time we wanted.

MRS BLACKITT: Really?

MR BLACKITT: Oh yes. And, what's more, because we don't believe in all that Papist claptrap we can take precautions.

MRS BLACKITT: What, you mean lock the door...?

MR BLACKITT: No, no. I mean because we are members of the Protestant Reformed Church which successfully challenged the autocratic power of the Papacy in the mid-sixteenth century we can wear little rubber devices to prevent issue.

MRS BLACKITT: What do you mean?

MR BLACKITT: I could, if I wanted, have sexual intercourse with you...

MRS BLACKITT: Oh, yes...Harry....

MR BLACKITT: And by wearing a rubber sheath over my old feller I could ensure that when I came off...you would not be impregnated.

MRS BLACKITT: Ooh!

MR BLACKITT: That's what being a Protestant's all about. That's why it's the church for me. That's why it's the church for anyone who respects the individual and the individual's right to decide for him or herself. When Martin Luther nailed his protest up to the church door in 1517, he may not have realised the full significance of what he was doing. But four hundred years later, thanks to him, my dear, I can wear whatever I want on my John Thomas. And Protestantism doesn't stop at the simple condom. Oh no! I can wear French Ticklers if I want.

MRS BLACKITT: You what?

MR BLACKITT: French Ticklers...Black Mambos...Crocodile Ribs...Sheaths that are designed not only to protect but also to enhance the stimulation of sexual congress....

MRS BLACKITT: Have you got one?

MR BLACKITT: Have I got one? Well no... But I can go down the road any time I want and walk into Harry's and hold my head up high, and say in a loud steady voice: 'Harry I want you to sell me a condom. In fact today I think I'll have a French Tickler, for I am a Protestant....'

MRS BLACKITT: Well why don't you?

MR BLACKITT: But they...they cannot. Because their church never made the great leap out of the Middle Ages, and the domination of alien episcopal supremacy.

THE
LUMBERJACK
SONG

BARBER: I didn't want to be a barber anyway. I wanted to be a lumberjack. Leaping from tree to tree as they float down the mighty rivers of British Columbia... The giant redwood, the larch, the fir, the mighty scots pine. *(a choir of Mounties is heard faintly in the distance)* The smell of fresh-cut timber! The crash of mighty trees! With my best girlie by my side... We'd sing...sing...sing.

I'm a lumberjack and I'm OK,
I sleep all night and I work all day.
MOUNTIES CHOIR: He's a lumberjack and he's OK,
He sleeps all night and he works all day.
BARBER: I cut down trees, I eat my lunch,
I go to the lavatory.
On Wednesdays I go shopping,
And have buttered scones for tea.

MOUNTIES CHOIR: He cuts down trees, he eats his lunch,
He goes to the lavatory.
On Wednesdays he goes shopping,
And has buttered scones for tea.
He's a lumberjack and he's OK,
He sleeps all night and he works all day.

BARBER: I cut down trees, I skip and jump,
I like to press wild flowers,
I put on women's clothing
And hang around in bars.

MOUNTIES CHOIR: He cuts down trees,
he skips and jumps,
He likes to press wild flowers.
He puts on women's clothing
And hangs around in bars...?
He's a lumberjack and he's OK,
He sleeps all night and he works all day.

BARBER: I cut down trees, I wear high heels,
Suspenders and a bra.
I wish I'd been a girlie,
Just like my dear Mama.
MOUNTIES CHOIR: He cuts down trees,
he wears high heels,
Suspenders...and a bra?...

GIRL: Oh Bevis! And I thought
you were so rugged.

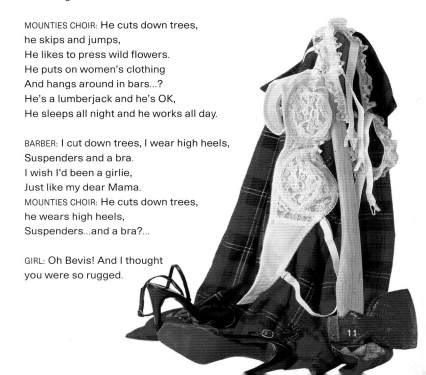

THE **PRODIGAL SON**
RETURNS

A sitting room straight out of D.H. Lawrence. Mum, wiping her hands on her arm and ushering in a young man in a suit.

MUM: Oh Dad...look who's come to see us...it's our Ken.

DAD *(without looking up)*: Aye, and about bloody time if you ask me.

KEN: Aren't you pleased to see me, Father?

MUM *(squeezing his arm reassuringly)*: Of course he's pleased to see you, Ken, he...

DAD: All right, woman, all right I've got a tongue in my head - I'll do t'talkin' *(looks at Ken distastefully)* Aye...I like yer fancy suit. Is that what their wearing up in Yorkshire now?

KEN: It's just an ordinary suit, father...it's all I've got apart from the overalls.

Dad turns away with an expression of scornful disgust.

MUM: How are you liking it down the mine, Ken?

KEN: Oh, it's not too bad, mum...we're using some new tungsten carbide drills for the preliminary coal-face scouring operations.

MUM: Oh that sounds nice, dear...

DAD: Tungsten carbide drills! What the bloody hell's tungsten carbide drills?

KEN: It's something they use in coal-mining, Father.

DAD *(mimicking)*: 'It's something they use in coal-mining, father'. You're all bloody fancy talk since you left London.

KEN: Oh not that again.

MUM *(to Ken)*: He's had a hard day dear...his new play opens at the National Theatre tomorrow.

KEN: Oh that's good.

DAD: Good! *good?* What do you know about it? What do you know about getting up at five o'clock in t'morning to fly to Paris...back at the Old Vic for drinks at twelve, sweating the day through press interviews, television interviews and getting back here at ten to wrestle with the problem of a homosexual nymphomaniac drug-addict involved in the ritual murder of a well known Scottish foot-baller. That's a full working day, lad, and don't you forget it!

MUM: Oh, don't shout at the boy, Father.

DAD: Aye, 'ampstead wasn't good enough for you, was it?...you had to go poncing off to Barnsley, you and yer coal-mining friends. *(spits)*

KEN: Coal-mining is a wonderful thing, Father, but it's something you'll never understand. Just look at you!

MUM: Oh Ken! Be careful! You know what he's like after a few novels.

DAD: Oh come on lad! Come on, out wi' it! What's wrong wi' me?...you *tit*!

KEN: I'll tell you what's wrong with you. Your head's addled with novels and poems, you come home every evening reeking of Château La Tour...

MUM: Oh don't, don't.

KEN: And look what you've done to mother! She's worn out with meeting film stars, attending premières and giving gala luncheons...

DAD: There's nowt wrong wi' gala luncheons, lad! I've had more gala luncheons than you've had hot dinners!

MUM: Oh please!

DAD: Aaaaaaagh! *(clutches hands and sinks to knees)*

MUM: Oh no!

KEN: What is it?

MUM: Oh, it's his writer's cramp!

KEN: You never told me about this...

MUM: No, we didn't like to, Kenny.

DAD: I'm all right! I'm all right, woman. Just get him out of here.

KEN: All right. I'm going.

DAD: After all we've done for him...

KEN *(at the door)*: One day you'll realize there's more to life than culture...There's dirt, and smoke, and good honest sweat!

DAD: Get out! Get out! Get OUT! You...LABOURER!

Ken goes. Shocked silence. Dad goes to table and takes the cover off the typewriter.

DAD: Hey, you know, mother, I think there's a play there...get t'agent on t'phone.

MUM: Aye I think you're right, Frank, it could express, it could express a vital theme of our age...

DAD: Aye.

THE NEWS FOR PARROTS

Good evening. Here is the News for parrots. No parrots were involved in an accident on the MI today, when a lorry carrying high octane fuel was in collision with a bollard...that is a *bollard* and not a *parrot*. A spokesman for parrots said he was glad no parrots were involved. The Minister of Technology today met the three Russian leaders to discuss a £4 million airliner deal... None of them went in the cage, or swung on the little wooden trapeze, or ate any of the nice millet seed, yum, yum. That's the end of the news. Now our programmes for parrots continue with part three of "A Tale of Two Cities" specially adapted for parrots by Joey Boy. The story so far...Dr Manette is in England after eighteen years in the Bastille. His daughter Lucy awaits her lover Charles Darnay who, we have just learned, is in fact the nephew of the Marquis de St Evremond, whose cruelty had placed Manette in the Bastille. Darnay arrives to find Lucy tending her aged father...

London 1793. *An eighteenth-century living room. Lucy is nursing her father. Suddenly the door bursts open and Charles Darnay enters.*

DARNAY: 'Allo, 'allo.
LUCY: 'Allo, 'allo, 'allo.
OLD MAN: 'Allo, 'allo, 'allo.
DARNAY: Who's a pretty boy then?

15

RAT
RECIPES

RAT PIE

Take four medium-sized rats and lay them on the chopping board.
Having first made sure the chopper is freshly sharpened, raise it as
high above the first rat as you can. Make sure that the rat's neck is
well exposed, then bring the chopper down with as much force as
possible onto the neck or head of the rat. Then cook it in a pie.

RAT SOUFFLÉ

Make sure that the rat's squeals are not audible from the street, par-
ticularly in areas where the Anti-Soufflé League and similar do-
gooders are out to persecute the innocent pleasures of the table.
Anyway, cut the rat down and lay it on the chopping board.
Raise the chopper high above your head, with the steel glinting in
the setting sun, and then bring it down - wham! - with a vivid crunch -
straight across the taut neck of the terrified rodent, and make it into
a soufflé.

Bits of rat hidden under a chair:
This isn't so much a recipe as a bit of advice in the event of members of the Anti-Soufflé League or its simpering lackeys breaking into your flat. Your wife (or a friend's) should engage the pusillanimous toadies from the League in conversation, perhaps turning the chat to the price of corn and the terrible damage inflicted by all kinds of rodents on personal property, and rats attacking small babies (this bit always takes the steam out of them) and you should have time to get any rat-bits safely out of sight. Incidentally, do make sure that your current copy of *The Rat Gourmet* hasn't been left lying around, otherwise all will be in vain, and the braying hounds of the culinary killjoys will be unleashed upon the things you cherish: your chopping board, the chopper caught in the blood-red glare of the fading sun. Bring it down - crunch! The slight splintering of the tiny spinal column under the keen metal! The last squeal and the death twitches of the helpless rat!

WHAT HAVE THE ROMANS EVER DONE FOR US?

The interior of Matthias's house. A cellar-like room with a very conspiratorial atmosphere.

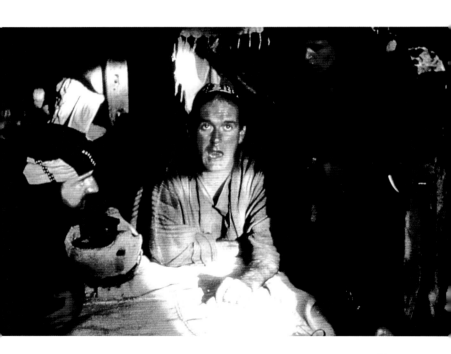

REG: They've bled us white, the bastards. They've taken everything we had, not just from us, from our fathers and from our fathers' fathers.

STAN: And from our fathers' fathers' fathers.

REG: Yes.

STAN: And our fathers' fathers' fathers' fathers.

REG: All right, Stan. Don't labour the point. And what have they ever given us in return?

He pauses smugly.

Voice from masked commando.

XERXES: The aqueduct?

REG: What?

XERXES: The aqueduct.

REG: Oh yeah, yeah, they gave us that. Yeah. That's true.

MASKED COMMANDO: And the sanitation!

STAN: Oh yes...sanitation, Reg, you remember what the city used to be like.

Murmurs of agreement.

REG: All right, I'll grant you that the aqueduct and the sanitation are two things that the Romans have done...

MATTHIAS: And the roads...

REG *(sharply)*: Well yes obviously the roads..the roads go without saying. But apart from the aqueduct, the sanitation and the roads...

ANOTHER MASKED COMMANDO: Irrigation...

OTHER MASKED VOICES: Medicine...Education...Health.

REG: Yes...all right, fair enough...

COMMANDO NEARER THE FRONT: And the wine...

GENERAL: Oh yes! True?

FRANCIS: Yeah. That's something we'd really miss if the Romans left, Reg.

MASKED COMMANDO AT BACK: Public baths!

STAN: And it's safe to walk in the streets at night now.

FRANCIS: Yes, they certainly know how to keep order...

General nodding.

...let's face it, they're the only ones who could in a place like this.

More general murmurs of agreement.

REG: All right...all right...but apart from better sanitation and medicine and education and irrigation and public health and roads and a freshwater system and baths and public order...what have the Romans done for us...?

XERXES: Brought peace!

REG *(very angry, he's not having a good meeting at all)*: What!? Oh...*(scornfully)* Peace, yes...shut up!

A PAGE FOR THOSE WHO LIKE FIGURES OF SPEECH

This is a page specially written for people who like figures of speech, for the not a few fans of litotes and those with no small interest in meiosis, for the infinite millions of hyperbole-lovers, for those fond of hypallage and the epithet's golden transfer, for those who fall willingly into the arms of the metaphor, those who give up the ghost, bury their heads in the sand and ride roughshod over the mixed metaphor, and even those of hyperbaton the friends. It will be too, for those who reprehend the malapropism; who love the wealth of metonymy; for all friends of rhetoric and syllepsis; and zeugmatists with smiling eyes and hearts. It will bring a large absence of unsatisfactory malevolence to periphrastic fans; a wig harm bello to spoonerists; and in no small measure a not less than splendid greeting to you circumlocutors. The World adores prosopopeiasts, and the friendly faces of synechdochists, and can one not make those amorous of anacoluthon understand that if they are not satisfied by this, what is to happen to them? It will attempt to really welcome all splitters of infinitives, all who are Romeo and Juliet to antonomasia, those who drink up similes like sparkling champagne, who lose nothing compared with comparison heads, self-evident axiomists, all pithy aphorists, apothegemists, maximiles, theorists, epigrammatists and even gnomists. And as for the lovers of aposiopeses...! It will wish bienvenu to all classical adherents of euphuism, all metathesistic birds, golden paronomasiasts covered in guilt, fallacious paralogists, trophists, anagogists, and anaphorists; to greet, welcome, embrace asyndeton buffs, while the lovers of ellipsis will be well-met and its followers embraced, as will be chronic worshippers of catachresis and supporters of anastrophe the world over.

FIND THE FISH

LADY TV PRESENTER: Hallo and welcome to
the Middle Of The Film. The moment where
we take a break and invite you, the audience, to join us, the film-
makers, in "Find The Fish". We're going to show you a scene from
another film and ask you to guess where the fish is. But if you think
you know, don't keep it to yourselves - YELL OUT - so that all the cin-
ema can hear you. So here we are with "Find The Fish".

MAN: I wonder where that fish has gone.
WOMAN: You did love it so.
You looked after it like a son.
MAN *(strangely):* And it went wherever I did go.
WOMAN: Is it in the cupboard?
AUDIENCE: Yes! No!
WOMAN: Wouldn't you like to know.
It was a lovely little fish.
MAN *(strangely):* And it went wherever I did go.
MAN IN AUDIENCE: It's behind the sofa!
An elephant joins the man and the woman.
WOMAN: Where can the fish be?
MAN IN AUDIENCE: Have you thought of the drawers in the bureau?
WOMAN: It is a most elusive fish.
MAN *(strangely):* And it went wherever I did go!
WOMAN: Oh fishy, fishy, fishy, fish.
MAN: Fish, fish, fish fishy oh!
WOMAN: Oh fishy, fishy, fishy, fish.
MAN *(strangely):* That went wherever I did go.

ALBATROSS

A man in an ice-cream girl's uniform is standing in a spotlight with an ice-cream tray with an albatross on it.

MAN: Albatross! Albatross! Albatross!
A person approaches him.
PERSON: Two choc-ices please.
MAN: I haven't got choc-ices. I only got the albatross. Albatross!
PERSON: What flavour is it?
MAN: It's a bird, innit. It's a bloody sea bird...it's not any bloody flavour. Albatross!
PERSON: Do you get wafers with it?
MAN: 'Course you don't get bloody wafers with it. Albatross!
PERSON: How much is it?
MAN: Ninepence.
PERSON: I'll have two please.
MAN: Gannet on a stick.

THE MERCHANT OF VENICE

PERFORMED BY THE DAIRY HERD OF BAD TOLTZ

It is always a joy to welcome a new interpretation of one of Shakespeare's works, but seldom do we find something so totally and refreshingly original as this production by the cows of Bad Toltz.

The Merchant of Venice has always been a difficult play for animals. I remember some chickens from Kaiserslauten having a shot at it three years ago, and failing miserably. But these cows have avoided all the pitfalls that the chickens fell into. They haven't tried to dress up, they haven't tried to make the play into an allegory about eggs, and they don't run away all the time. I loved it. And I can't wait to see these fine dairy cows get to grips with Wagner at Bayreuth next week.

MADAME PALM WRITES

Dear Madame Palm,
Our Local Building Society Branch Manager says that Insurance is illegal. Can this be true?
Ron Higgins, Cirencester.

Dear Ron, there is absolutely no need to be ashamed of your body. Sex is a perfectly natural function that all post-pubescent people indulge in. For heavens sake can't we get it out in the open?

Dear Madame Palm,
What can I do about acne? I have tried everything, creams, jellies, injections, pumice stone, dieting, tablets and mud packs, but no matter what I do my skin remains smooth and clear. Can you buy acne?
Yours hopefully,
R. Bradshaw, Biggleswade.

Dear R. Bradshaw, please believe me when I tell you that sex is absolutely normal for people of all ages and between everybody and anyone except filthy perverts who should be castrated and locked away for ever, honestly, hanging is too good for them. Love and understanding will go a long way towards curing all the ills in the world except nasty filthy perverts who should be put down at once.

Dear Madame Palm,
Can you settle a family argument? My parents say that black and white television is really in colour, but I maintain that colour TV is really black and white. Who is right?
Puzzled, Wakefield.

Dear Puzzled, sex is one of God's greatest gifts, along with nudity, golf and wrestling. Please try and understand that no matter how dirty your desires may seem they are perfectly natural.
P.S. I am sending you some leaflets. Good aren't they?

SPAM

*A café. All the customers are Vikings. Mr and Mrs Bun
enter - downwards.*

MR BUN: Morning.

WAITRESS: Morning.

MR BUN: What have you got, then?

WAITRESS: Well there's egg and bacon; egg, sausage and bacon; egg
and spam; egg, bacon and spam; egg, bacon, sausage and spam;
spam, bacon sausage and spam; spam, egg, spam, spam, bacon and
spam; spam, spam, spam, egg and spam; spam, spam, spam, spam,
spam, spam, baked beans, spam, spam, spam, and spam; or lobster
thermidor aux crevettes with a mornay sauce garnished with truffle
pâté, brandy and a fried egg on top and spam.

MRS BUN: Have you got anything without spam in it?

WAITRESS: Well, there's spam, egg, sausage and spam. That's not got
much spam in it.

MRS BUN: I don't want *any* spam.

MR BUN: Why can't she have egg, bacon spam and sausage?

MRS BUN: That's got spam in it!

MR BUN: Not as much as spam, egg, sausage and spam.

MRS BUN: Look, could I have egg, bacon, spam and sausage without
the spam.

WAITRESS: Uuuuuuggggh!

MRS BUN: What d'you mean uuugggh! I don't like spam.

VIKINGS *(singing)*: Spam, spam, spam, spam, spam...spam, spam,
spam, spam...lovely spam, wonderful spam...

WAITRESS: Shut up. Shut up! Shut up! You can't have egg, bacon, spam
and sausage without the spam.

MRS BUN: Why not?

WAITRESS: No, it wouldn't be egg, bacon, spam and sausage, would it.

MRS BUN: I don't like spam!

MR BUN: Don't make a fuss, dear. I'll have your spam. I love it. I'm having spam, spam, spam, spam, spam...

VIKINGS *(singing)*: Spam, spam, spam, spam...

MR BUN: ...baked beans, spam, spam and spam.

WAITRESS: Baked beans are off.

MR BUN: Well can I have spam instead?

WAITRESS: You mean spam, spam, spam, spam, spam, spam, spam, spam, spam, spam?

VIKINGS *(still singing)*: Spam, spam, spam, spam...

MR BUN: Yes.

WAITRESS: Arrggh!

VIKINGS: ...lovely spam, wonderful, spam.

WAITRESS: Shut up! Shut up!

Superimposed caption: "A Historian"

HISTORIAN: Another great Viking victory was at the Green Midget café at Bromley. Once again the Viking strategy was the same. They sailed from these fiords here *(indicating a map with arrows on it)*, assembled at Trondheim and waited for the strong north-easterly winds to blow their oaken galleys to England whence they sailed on May 23rd. Once in Bromley they assembled in the Green Midget café and spam selecting a spam particular spam item from the spam menu would spam, spam, spam, spam, spam...

The backdrop behind him rises to reveal the café again. The Vikings start singing again and the historian conducts them.

VIKINGS *(singing)*: Spam, spam, spam, spam, spam, lovely spam, wonderful spam. Lovely spam, wonderful spam.

CONSTITUTIONAL
PEASANTS

KING ARTHUR *and his squire* PATSY *overtake a* PEASANT *pulling a cart towards a distant castle.*

ARTHUR: Old woman!

DENNIS: *(turning)*: Man.

ARTHUR: Man. I'm sorry. Old man, what knight lives in that castle?

DENNIS: I'm thirty-seven.

ARTHUR: What?

DENNIS: I'm only thirty-seven...I'm not old.

ARTHUR: Well - I can't just say: "Hey, Man!"

DENNIS: You could say: "Dennis".

ARTHUR: I didn't know you were called Dennis.

DENNIS: You didn't bother to find out, did you?

ARTHUR: I've said I'm sorry about the old woman, but from behind you looked...

DENNIS: What I object to is that you automatically treat me as an inferior...

ARTHUR: Well...I am King.

DENNIS: Oh, very nice. King, eh! I expect you've got a palace and fine clothes and courtiers and plenty of food. And how d'you get that? By exploiting the workers! By hanging onto outdated imperialistic dogma, which perpetuates the social and economic differences in our society! If there's ever going to be any progress...

An OLD WOMAN *appears*.

OLD WOMAN: Dennis! There's some lovely filth down here...Oh! How d'you do?

ARTHUR: How d'you do, good lady...I am Arthur, King of the Britons...can you tell me who lives in that castle?

OLD WOMAN: King of the who?

ARTHUR: The Britons.

OLD WOMAN: Who are the Britons?

ARTHUR: All of us are...we are all Britons. (DENNIS *winks at the* OLD

WOMAN)...And I am your King...

OLD WOMAN: Ooooh! I didn't know we had a king. I thought we were an autonomous collective...

DENNIS: You're fooling yourself. We're living in a dictatorship, a self-perpetuating autocracy in which the working classes...

OLD WOMAN: There you are, bringing class into it again...

DENNIS: That's what it's all about...If only...

ARTHUR: Please, please, good people, I am in haste. What knight lives in that castle?

OLD WOMAN: No one lives there.

ARTHUR: Well, who is your lord?

OLD WOMAN: We don't have a lord.

ARTHUR: What?

DENNIS: I told you, we're an anarcho-syndicalist commune, we take it in turns to act as a sort of executive officer for the week.

ARTHUR: Yes...

DENNIS: ...But all the decisions of that officer...

ARTHUR: Yes, I see.

DENNIS: ...must be approved at a bi-weekly meeting by a simple majority in the case of purely internal affairs...

ARTHUR: Be quiet.

DENNIS: But a two-thirds majority...

ARTHUR: Be quiet! I order you to shut up.

OLD WOMAN: Order, eh? Who does he think he is?

ARTHUR: I am your King.

OLD WOMAN: Well, I didn't vote for you.

ARTHUR: You don't vote for kings.

OLD WOMAN: Well, how did you become King, then?

ARTHUR: The Lady of the Lake, her arm clad in purest shimmering samite, held Excalibur aloft from the bosom of the waters to signify that by Divine Providence...I, Arthur, was to carry Excalibur...that is why I am your King.

DENNIS: Look, strange women lying on their backs in ponds handing over swords...that's no basis for a system of government. Supreme executive power derives from a mandate from the masses not from some farcical aquatic ceremony.

ARTHUR: Be quiet!

DENNIS: You can't expect to wield supreme executive power just because some watery tart threw a sword at you.

ARTHUR: Shut up!

DENNIS: I mean, if I went around saying I was an Emperor because some moistened bint had lobbed a scimitar at me, people would put me away.

ARTHUR *(grabbing him by the collar)*: Shut up, will you. Shut up!

DENNIS: Ah! *Now*...we see the violence inherent in the system.

...EVERY SPERM IS SACRED

There are Jews in the world,
There are Buddhists,
There are Hindus and Mormons and then,
There are those that follow Mohammed,
But I've never been one of them...
I'm a Roman Catholic,
And have been since before I was born,
And the one thing they say about Catholics,
Is they'll take you as soon as you're warm...
You don't have to be a six-footer,
You don't have to have a great brain,
You don't have to have any clothes on
You're a Catholic the moment Dad came...
Because...

Every sperm is sacred,
Every sperm is great,
If a sperm is wasted,
God gets quite irate.

Let the heathen spill theirs,
On the dusty ground,
God shall make them pay for
Each sperm that can't be found.

Every sperm is wanted,
Every sperm is good,
Every sperm is needed
In your neighbourhood.

35

Hindu, Taoist, Mormon,
Spill theirs just anywhere,
But God loves those who treat their
Semen with more care.

Every sperm is sacred,
Every sperm is great,
If a sperm is wasted
God gets quite irate.

Every sperm is sacred,
Every sperm is good,
Every sperm is needed
In your neighbourhood.

Every sperm is useful,
Every sperm is fine,
God needs everybody's,
Mine!
And mine!
And mine!

Let the pagan spill theirs,
O'er mountain, hill and plain,
God shall strike them down for
Each sperm that's spilt in vain.

Every sperm is sacred,
Every sperm is good,
Every sperm is needed
In your neighbourhood.

Every sperm is sacred,
Every sperm is great,
If a sperm is wasted,
God gets quite irate.

THE UNDERTAKER
SKETCH

An undertaker's shop.

UNDERTAKER: Morning.

MAN: Good morning.

UNDERTAKER: What can I do for you, squire?

MAN: Well, I wonder if you can help me. You see, my mother has just died.

UNDERTAKER: Ah well, we can help you. We deal with stiffs.

MAN: What?

UNDERTAKER: Well, there's three things we can do with your mum. We can burn her, bury her or dump her.

MAN *(shocked)*: Dump her?

UNDERTAKER: Dump her in the Thames.

MAN: What?

UNDERTAKER: Oh, did you like her?

MAN: Yes!

UNDERTAKER: Oh well, we won't dump her, then. Well what do you think? We can bury her or burn her.

MAN: Well, which do you recommend?

UNDERTAKER: Well, they're both nasty. If we burn her she gets stuffed in the flames, crackle, crackle, crackle, which is a bit of a shock if she's not quite dead, but quick, and then we give you a handful of ashes, which you can pretend were hers.

MAN: Oh.

UNDERTAKER: Or if we bury her she gets eaten up by lots of weevils, and nasty maggots, which as I said before is a bit of a shock if she's not quite dead.

MAN: I see. Well, she's definitely dead.

UNDERTAKER: Where is she?

MAN: She's in this sack.

UNDERTAKER: Can I have a look? She looks quite young.

MAN: Yes, yes, she was.

UNDERTAKER *(calling)*: Fred!

FRED'S VOICE: Yeah?

UNDERTAKER: I think we've got an eater.

MAN: What?

Another undertaker pokes his head round the door.

FRED: Right, I'll get the oven on. *(He goes off)*

MAN: Er, excuse me, um, are you suggesting eating my mother?

UNDERTAKER: Er...yeah, not raw. Cooked.

MAN: What?

UNDERTAKER: Yes, roasted with a few french fries, broccoli, horseradish sauce...

MAN: Well, I do feel a bit peckish.

UNDERTAKER: Great!

MAN: Can we have some parsnips?

UNDERTAKER *(calling)*: Fred - get some parsnips.

MAN: I really don't think I should.

UNDERTAKER: Look, tell you what, we'll eat her; if you feel a bit guilty about it after, we can dig a grave and you can throw up in it.

Dear Sir or Madame Palm,
I, or rather a friend of mine,
although I suppose I might as
well be honest and say straight
out that it is really me, but it
may not be me. I could have a
friend like it as well, but no! To
be honest, it is me, suffer from
indecision. Probably.

I have lost two or three or
perhaps five jobs in the last day
or days. Please tell me what to
do. No, no, don't. Yours faithfully
or sincerely, Stephen or Mavis
Buchanan,or Jack Noonan.

Dear All, no of course you can't
get pregnant that way.

Dear Madame Palm.
Our dog Nipper has just won a
seat in the U.S. Senate. Will he
have to be vaccinated? Yours,
Y.Wilcox, Preston.

Yes Mr Wilcox, I'm afraid all
U.S. Senators have to be
vaccinated.

Dear Madame Palm,
I served for eight years with the
Ghurkas. We fought against
incredible odds in all parts of
the North Western Frontier to
safeguard the freedom and the
right to self-determination of
the people of Southern Asia. I
am now a part-time notice
board in a prominent public
school. I also prefer wearing
women's dresses. Are there
anyother ex-Ghurkas similarly
interested?NAME AND RANK
SUPPLIED.

Dear Name and Rank
Supplied, what a lovely
name. No of course you
shouldn't give up. Try taking
a hot bath first to relax
yourself and then keep trying.
Don't worry if it doesn't work
at first, it'll soon become fun
and practice makes perfect,
as the doctors say.
There's nothing better than
a jolly good

THE MAN WHO TALKS ENTIRELY IN ANAGRAMS

INTERVIEWER: Hello, good evening and welcome to another edition of "Blood, Devastation, Death, War and Horror", and later on we'll be talking to a man who *does* gardening. But our first guest in the studio tonight is a man who talks entirely in anagrams.

MAN: Taht si crreoct.

INTERVIEWER: Do you enjoy this?

MAN: I stom certainly od. Revy chum so.

INTERVIEWER: And what's your name?

MAN: Hamrag. Hamrag Yatlerot.

INTERVIEWER: Well, Graham, nice to have you on the show. Now where do you come from?

MAN: Bumcreland.

INTERVIEWER: Cumberland?

MAN: Staht sit sepreicly.

INTERVIEWER: And I believe you're working on an anagram version of Shakespeare...

MAN: Sey, sey, taht si crreoct, er. Ta mnemot I'm wroking on *The Mating of the Wersh*.

INTERVIEWER: *The Mating of the Wersh*. By William Shakespeare?

MAN: Nay, by Malliwi Rapesheake.

INTERVIEWER: And er, what else?

MAN: *Two Netlemeg of Verona*, *Twelfth Thing*, *The Chamrent of Venice*...

INTERVIEWER: Have you done *Hamlet*?

MAN: *Thamle*. "Be ot or bot ne ot, tath is the nestquie".

INTERVIEWER: And what is your next project?

MAN: *Ring Kichard the Thrid*

INTERVIEWER: I'm sorry?

MAN: "A shroe! A shroe! My dingkome for a shroe!"

INTERVIEWER: Ah, Ring Kichard, yes...but surely that's not an anagram, that's a spoonerism.

MAN: If you're going to split hairs I'm going to piss off.

chez rat

chez rat

Hors D'Oeuvres

Soup of the Day (nearly always rat)

Melon Venezia (succulent honeydew melon, soaked in Kirsch, with a dead rat on top)

Ratatouille

Escargot (really rat)

Entrées

Rat au Vin (fresh rat killed with a chopper held up against the glinting sunlight and brought down with a terrific wham! on the tiny vertebrate in wine)

Rat au Poivre (the same only more violent)

Rat à Tué (unlimited rats killed at your table by the method of your own choice)

Rat Muré (large black rats hurled at a wall by the chef)

Dessert

Rats (various)

Coffee and rats 40p extra

chez rat

"Somewhere in England, 1944". The squadron leader enters an RAF officers' mess and takes off his helmet.

BOVRIL: Morning, Squadron Leader.

SQUADRON LEADER: What-ho, Squiffy.

BOVRIL: How was it?

SQUADRON LEADER: Top hole. Bally Jerry pranged his kite right in the how's your father. Hairy blighter, dicky-birdied, feathered back on his Sammy, took a waspy, flipped over his Betty Harper's and caught his can in the Bertie.

BOVRIL: Er, I'm afraid I don't quite follow you, Squadron Leader.

SQUADRON LEADER: It's perfectly ordinary banter, Squiffy. Bally Jerry...pranged his kite, right in the how's yer father...hairy blighter, dicky-birdied, feathered back on his Sammy, took a waspy, flipped over on his Betty Harper's and caught his can in the Bertie.

BOVRIL: No, I'm just not understanding banter at all well today. Give us it slower.

SQUADRON LEADER: Banter's not the *same* if you say it slower, Squiffy.

BOVRIL: Hold on, then. *(shouts)* Wingco!

WINGCO: Yes!

BOVRIL: Bend an ear to the Squadron Leader's banter for a sec, would you?

WINGCO: Can do.

BOVRIL: Jolly good.

WINGCO: Fire away.

SQUADRON LEADE: *(draws a deep breath and looks slightly uncertain, then starts even more deliberately than before)*: Bally Jerry...pranged his kite...right in the how's yer father...hairy blighter...dicky-birdied...feathered back on his Sammy...took a waspy...flipped over

47

his Betty Harper's... and caught his can in the Bertie...

WINGCO: ...No, don't understand that banter at all.

SQUADRON LEADER: Something up with my banter, chaps?

A siren goes. The door bursts open and an out-of-breath young pilot rushes in in his flying gear.

PILOT: Bunch of monkeys on the ceiling, sir! Grab your egg and fours and let's get the bacon delivered.

General incomprehension. They look at each other.

WINGCO: Do you understand that?

SQUADRON LEADER: No, didn't get a word of it.

WINGCO: Sorry old man, we don't understand your banter.

PILOT: You know...bally ten-penny ones dropping in the custard...*(searching for the words)* um...Charlie Choppers chucking a handful...

WINGCO: No, no...sorry.

BOVRIL: Say it a bit slower, old chap.

PILOT: Slower banter, sir?

WINGCO: Ra-ther!

PILOT: Um...sausage squad up the blue end!

SQUADRON LEADER: No, still don't get it.

PILOT: Um...cabbage crates coming over the briny?

SQUADRON LEADER: No.

OTHERS: No, no...

VOICE OVER: But by then it was too late. The first cabbage crates hit London on July 7th. That was just the beginning...

THE OXFOD SIMPLIFIED
DICTIONARY

A

A a

Aard-vark a very difficult word which you don't need to know.

Abacinate another word which is totally useless and you won't ever use so don't go fretting over it or looking it up in another dictionary because honestly its pointless

Aback aback

Abacus a very similar word to "Aback".

Abalone *see* "Aard-vark"

Abandon to abandon

Abbey an abbey

Abbot an abbot

Abbreviate to abbreviate

Abdicate to abdicate

Abdication ditto near enough

Abditory also similar

Abdomen same again except for five letters

Abduct almost the same

Aberration an almost totally different word - ignore it

Abettor abdomen

Abeyance *see* "Aard-vark"

Knickers ladies' underpants

Abhorrent I wouldn't worry about what this word means

Abide abdicate

Abigail lady's maid

Ability ability

Abject abdicate

Abjure abject (only three letters' difference and they try to pass it off as a different word! Just shows those mealy-mouthed egg-heads in the universities haven't got anything better to do than split hairs over tiny little details that don't make a fart of difference to people's lives. Abject/abjure what's the difference? Who cares anyway?)

Ablative This kind of thing makes me sick! Does it matter a tinker's cuss what different endings they used to have in a language nobody speaks any more.

Ablaze ablaze

Able able

Abnegate to abjure! (It really is! Look it up in the O.E.D. if you don't believe me!)

Abnormal abnormal

Aboard aboard

Abode abode

Abolish abolish (this is what dictionaries ought to be like)

Abominable abominable

Abound abound

About about

Above above

Abracadabra abracadabra

Hey presto! hey presto!

Shazam! shazam!

Oogie-woogie it's a boogie

Abreast *not* "a breast"

Abroad practically the same as "Aboard" - in fact it's just got one tiny weeny little letter in a different place and they try to pass it off as a different word! Therefore, very definitely, *see* "Aboard".

Abrupt abrupt

Abscess a collection of pus or purulent matter formed by a morbid process in a cavity of the body. Great! It's words like that that make a dictionary really worthwhile.

Absolute absolute

Absolution absolute

Absolutist absolute

Absolutory absolute

Absolve absolute

Absonant absolute

Absorb absolute

Abstract abstract

Abuse abuse

Abyss abyss

Acadialte oh piss off.

B

Buttock buttock

Bum bum

Tit tit

This is the end of the "Oxfod Simplified Dictionary". Words beginning with the letter C onwards are seldom used, and are hardly worth including in a genuine simplified dictionary. N.B. We do not refund money to clever-dicks who want to look up other words. So there. Ed.

THE MINISTER FOR
NOT LISTENING TO PEOPLE

The Minister for not listening to people toured Batley today to investigate allegations of victimization in home-loan improvement grants, made last week by the Shadow Minister for judging people at first sight to be marginally worse than they actually are. At the Home Office, the Minister for inserting himself in between chairs and walls in men's clubs, was at his desk after a short illness. He spent the morning dealing with the Irish situation and later in the day had long discussions with the Minister for running upstairs two at a time, flinging the door open and saying "Ha, ha! Caught you, Mildred". In the Commons there was another day of heated debate on the third reading of the Trade Practices Bill. Mr Roland Penrose, the Under-Secretary for making deep growling noises grrr, launched a bitter personal attack on the ex-Minister for delving deep into a black satin bag and producing a tube of Euthymol toothpaste. Later in the debate the Junior Minister for being frightened by any kind of farm machinery, challenged the Under-Secretary of State for hiding from Terence Rattigan to produce the current year's trading figures, as supplied by the Department of stealing packets of bandages from the self-service counter at Timothy Whites and selling them again at a considerable profit. Parliament rose at 11.30, and, crawling along a dark passageway into the old rectory broke down the door to the serving hatch, painted the spare room and next weekend I think they'll be able to make a start on the boy's bedroom, while Amy and Roger, up in London for a few days, go to see the mysterious Mr Grenville.

THE COURT MARTIAL OF SAPPER WALTERS

A courtroom in the 1940s. A court martial is in progress. An elderly general presides, with two others on either side of him. There is a defence counsel, a prosecutor, a clerk of court, and two men guarding the prisoner.

PRESIDING GENERAL: Sapper Walters, you stand before this court accused of carrying on the war by other than warlike means - to wit, that you did on April 16th, 1942, dressed up as a bag of dainties, flick wet towels at the enemy during an important offensive...

WALTERS: Well, sir...

PRESIDING GENERAL: Shut up! Colonel Fawcett for the prosecution...

FAWCETT: Sir, we all know...

PRESIDING GENERAL: Shut up!

FAWCETT: I'm sorry?

PRESIDING GENERAL: Carry on.

FAWCETT: Sir, we all know the facts of the case; that Sapper Walters, being in possession of expensive military equipment, to wit one Lee Enfield .303 Rifle and 72 rounds of ammunition, valued at a hundred and forty pounds three shillings and sixpence, chose instead to use wet towels to take an enemy company post in the area of Basingstoke...

PRESIDING GENERAL: Basingstoke? Basingstoke in Hampshire?

FAWCETT: No, no, no, sir, no.

PRESIDING GENERAL: I see, carry on.

FAWCETT: The result of his action was that the enemy...

PRESIDING GENERAL: Basingstoke *where?*

FAWCETT: Basingstoke, Westphalia, sir.

PRESIDING GENERAL: Oh I *see*. Carry on.

FAWCETT: The result of Sapper Walter's action was that the enemy received wet patches upon their trousers and in some cases small red strawberry marks upon their thighs...

PRESIDING GENERAL: I didn't know there *was* a Basingstoke in Westphalia.

FAWCETT *(slightly irritated)*: It's on the map, sir.

PRESIDING GENERAL: What map?

FAWCETT *(more irritably)*: The map of Westphalia as used by the army, sir.

PRESIDING GENERAL: Well, I've certainly never heard of Basingstoke in Westphalia.

FAWCETT *(patiently)*: It's a municipal borough, sir, twenty-seven miles north north east of Southampton. Its chief manufactures...

PRESIDING GENERAL: What...Southampton in Westphalia?

FAWCETT: Yes sir...bricks...clothing. Nearby are the remains of Basing House, burned down by Cromwell's cavalry in 1645...

PRESIDING GENERAL: Who compiled this map?

FAWCETT: Cole Porter, sir.

PRESIDING GENERAL *(incredulously)*: Cole Porter...who wrote *Kiss Me Kate?*

FAWCETT: No, alas not, sir...this was Cole Porter who wrote "Anything Goes". Sir, I shall seek to prove that the man before this court...

PRESIDING GENERAL: That's the same one!

(he sings) "In olden days a glimpse of stocking…"

FAWCETT: I *beg* your pardon, sir?

PRESIDING GENERAL *(singing)*: "In olden days a glimpse of stocking, was looked on as something shocking, now heaven knows, anything goes…"

FAWCETT: No, this one's different, sir.

PRESIDING GENERAL: How does it go?

FAWCETT: What, sir?

PRESIDING GENERAL: How does *your* "Anything Goes" go?

WALTERS: Can I go home now?

PRESIDING GENERAL: Shut up! *(to Fawcett)* Come on!

FAWCETT: Sir, really, this is rather…

PRESIDING GENERAL: Come on, how does your "Anything Goes" go?

FAWCETT *(clearing his throat and going into an extraordinary tuneless and very loud song)*

> Anything goes in.
> Anything goes out!
> Fish, bananas, old pyjamas,
> Mutton! Beef! and Trout!
> Anything goes in…

PRESIDING GENERAL: No, that's not it…carry on.

FAWCETT: With respect sir, I shall seek to prove that the man before you in the dock, being in possession of the following: one pair of army boots, value three pounds seven and six, one pair of serge trousers, value two pounds three and six, one pair of gaiters value sixty-eight pounds ten shillings, one…

PRESIDING GENERAL: Sixty-eight pounds ten shillings for a pair of *gaiters*?

FAWCETT *(dismissively)*: They were special gaiters, sir.

PRESIDING GENERAL: *Special* gaiters?

FAWCETT: Yes sir, they were made in France. One beret costing fourteen shillings, one pair of...

PRESIDING GENERAL: What was so special about them?

FAWCETT: Oh...*(as if he can hardly be bothered to reply)* they were made of a special fabric, sir. The buckles were made of empire silver instead of brass. The total value of the uniform was there...

PRESIDING GENERAL: Why was the accused wearing special gaiters?

FAWCETT *(irritably)*: They were a presentation pair, from the regiment. The total value of the uniform...

PRESIDING GENERAL: Why did they present him with a special pair of gaiters?

FAWCETT: Sir, it seems to me totally irrelevant to the case whether the gaiters were presented to him or not, sir.

PRESIDING GENERAL: I think the court will be able to judge that for themselves. I want to know why the regiment presented the accused with a special pair of gaiters.

FAWCETT *(stifling his impatience)*: He...used to do things for them. The total value...

PRESIDING GENERAL: What things?

FAWCETT *(exasperated)*: He...used to oblige them, sir. The total value...

PRESIDING GENERAL: *Oblige* them?

FAWCETT: Yes sir. The total value of the uniform...

PRESIDING GENERAL: How did he *oblige* them?

FAWCETT *(more and more irritated)*: He...um...he used to make them happy in little ways, sir. The total value of the uniform could therefore not have been less than...

PRESIDING GENERAL: Did he touch them at all?

FAWCETT: Sir! I submit that this is totally irrelevant.

PRESIDING GENERAL: I want to know how he made them happy.

FAWCETT *(losing his temper)*: He used to ram things up their...

PRESIDING GENERAL *(quickly)*: All right! All right! No need to spell it out! What er...what has the accused got to say?

WALTERS *(taken off guard)*: What, me?

PRESIDING GENERAL: Yes. What have you got to say?

WALTERS: What can I say? I mean, how can I encapsulate in mere words my scorn for any military solution? The futility of modern warfare? And the hypocrisy by which contemporary government applies one standard to violence within the community and another to violence perpetrated by one community upon another?

DEFENCE COUNSEL: I'm sorry, but my client has become pretentious. I will say in his defence that he has suffered...

FAWCETT: Sir! We haven't finished the prosecution!

PRESIDING COUNSEL: Shut up! I'm in charge of this court. *(to the court)* Stand up! *(everyone stands up)* Sit down! *(everyone sits down)* Go moo! *(everyone goes moo; the presiding general turns to Fawcett)* See? Right, now, on with the pixie hats! *(everyone puts on pixie hats with large pointed ears)* And order in the skating vicar. *(a skating vicar enters and everyone bursts into song)*

EVERYONE: Anything goes in.
              Anything goes out!
              Fish, bananas, old pyjamas,
              Mutton! Beef! and Trout!
              Anything goes in.
              Anything goes out
              Fish, bananas, old pyjamas,
              Mutton! Beef! and Trout!

WHAT THE ST★RS REALLY SAY

MRS O: Morning Mrs Trepidatious.

MRS TREPIDATIOUS: Oh, I don't know what's good about it, my right arm's hanging off something awful.

MRS O: Oh, you want to have that seen to.

MRS TREPIDATIOUS: What, by that Dr Morrison? He's killed more patients than I've had severe boils.

MRS O: What do the stars say?

MRS TREPIDATIOUS: Well, Petula Clark says burst them early, but David Frost...

MRS O: No, the stars in the paper, you cloth-eared heap of anteater's catarrh, the zodiacal signs, the horoscopic fates, the astrological portents, the omens, the genethliac prognostications, the mantological harbingers, the vaticinal utterances, the fratridical premonitory uttering of the mantological omens - what do the bleeding stars in the paper predict, forecast, prophesy, foretell, prognosticate...

A big sheet is lowered with the words on

VOICE OVER: And this is where you at home can join in.

MRS O: ...forebode, bode, augur, spell, foretoken, presage, portend, foreshow, foreshadow, forerun, herald, point to, betoken, indicate!

MRS TREPIDATIOUS: I don't know.

The sheet is raised again

MRS O: What are you?

MRS TREPIDATIOUS: I'm Nesbitt.

MRS O: There's not a zodiacal sign called Nesbitt.

MRS TREPIDATIOUS: All right, Derry and Toms.

MRS O *(surveying the paper)*: Aquarius, Scorpio, Virgo, Derry and Toms. April 29th to March 22nd. Even dates only.

MRS TREPIDATIOUS: Well what does it presage?

MRS O: You have green, scaly skin, and a soft yellow underbelly with a series of fin-like ridges running down your spine and tail. Although lizardlike in shape, you can grow anything up to thirty feet in length with huge teeth that can bite off great rocks and trees. You inhabit arid sub-tropical zones and wear spectacles.

MRS TREPIDATIOUS: It's very good about the spectacles.

MRS O: It's amazing.

MRS TREPIDATIOUS: Mm...what's yours, Irene?

MRS O: Basil.

MRS TREPIDATIOUS: I'm sorry, what's yours, Basil?

MRS O: No. That's my star sign, Basil...

MRS TREPIDATIOUS: There isn't a...

MRS O: Yes there is...Aquarius, Sagittarius, Derry and Toms, Basil. June 21st to June 22nd.

MRS TREPIDATIOUS: Well, what does it say?

MRS O: You have green, scaly skin and a series of yellow underbellies running down your spine and tail...

MRS TREPIDATIOUS: That's exactly the same!

MRS O: Try number one...what's Aquarius?

MRS TREPIDATIOUS: It's a zodiacal sign.

MRS O: I know that, what does it say in the paper Mrs Flan-and-pickle?

MRS TREPIDATIOUS: All right...Oh! It says, "a wonderful day ahead". You will be surrounded by family and friends. Roger Moore will drop in for lunch, bringing Tony Curtis with him. In the afternoon a substantial cash sum will come your way. In the evening Petula Clark will visit your home accompanied by the Mike Sammes singers. She will sing for you in your own living room. Before you go to bed, Peter Wyngarde will come and declare his undying love for you.

MRS O: Urghh! What's Scorpio?

MRS TREPIDATIOUS: Oh, that's very good. "You will have lunch with a school-friend of Duane Eddy's, who will insist on whistling some of Duane's greatest instrumental hits. In the afternoon you will die, you will be buried..."

THE GALAXY
SONG

And revolving at nine hundred miles an hour,
That's orbiting at nineteen miles a second, so it's reckoned,
A sun that is the source of all our power.
The sun and you and me and all the stars that we can see,
Are moving at a million miles a day
In an outer spiral arm, at forty thousand miles an hour,
Of the galaxy we call the Milky Way.

Our galaxy itself contains a hundred billion stars
It's a hundred thousand light years side to side.
It bulges in the middle sixteen thousand light years thick
But out by us its just three thousand light years wide
We're thirty thousand light years from galactic central point,
We go round every two hundred million years
And our galaxy is only one of millions of billions
In this amazing and expanding Universe.

The Universe itself keeps expanding and expanding
In all of the directions it can whizz
As fast as it can go, at the speed of light you know,
Twelve million miles a minute, and that's the fastest speed there is.
So remember when you're feeling very small and insecure
How amazingly unlikely is your birth
And pray that there's intelligent life somewhere up in space
Because there's bugger all down here on earth.

BIBLIOGRAPHY

If you enjoyed this book here are a few more books that you may enjoy but probably not.

Non-Fiction
The Boys' Book of Burglary
Breaking and Entering For Beginners
Do's and Don'ts For the First-Time House- Breaker
Violent Intrusion Made Easy
A Primer of Larceny With Menaces
Why Have Locks?
The Evils of Home Security Systems
Why You Should Never Bolt Your Doors
The Practical Home-Builder's Manual Number Five: Leaving Valuables About For All to See When They Look In Your Windows
Burglars Have to Live Too
Neighbourhood Watch (A Tale of Treachery and Horror)
My Burglar, My Friend
Why It Makes Sense To Spryzgee
The A to Z of B To Y
The Royal Britannia Encyclopaedia of Very Small Holes Made In Metal Surfaces By Certain Kinds of Filament Under Certain Conditions (not recommended)
The Bumper Book of Very Easy Facts Made Very Simple For People With Very Small Brains
The Bumper Book of Very Easy Facts Made Very Simple For People With Very Small Brains But With Pictures of Girls With Large Breasts (A *Sun* Special)
Raspberryade - The Extraordinary Exposé
Raspberryade - An Apology
Raspberryade - The True Story Behind the Revelations Scandal

Raspberryade - At Last! The True Facts!
Raspberryade - What Was it All About?
The Wonderful World of Chicken Sexing
How To Turn Unwanted Clothing Into Pastrami Sandwiches
The Art of Cooking With Motor Oil
Cooking With Poisonous Mushrooms (Ideal for those who hate cooking for
    friends)
Cooking Delia Smith
Cooking With Delia Smith - (Contains an Apology for the previous edition)
Eating Well - Drinking Badly - A Guide To Thoroughly Enjoying Yourself
Eating Well - Drinking Badly - Throwing-up Often (sequel)
The Air-Hostesses' Guide To Passengers Who Are Looking For A One -Night Stand
*The Air-Hostesses' Guide To Male Passengers Who Are Looking For A
    One-Night Stand With No Strings And No Exchange of Addresses*
*The Air-Hostesses' Guide To Wealthy Male Passengers Who Are Looking
    For A One-Night Stand But May Be Willing To Turn It Into A Longer Term
    Relationship Though Without Committing To Any Binding Financial
    Arrangement After Only One Night - Understandably*
*The Air- Hostesses' Guide To Passengers Who Are Looking For A One-
    Night Stand On Condition That They Can Also Speak To The Pilot First*
*The Air- Hostesses' Guide To Passengers Who Are Looking For A One-Night
    Stand Without Necessarily Being Interested in Sex But Just Good Company
    And A Few Laughs And Maybe Some Pickles And A Banana Before Pissing
    Off To Their Own Hotel Room*
The Air-Hostesses' Guide To Hot-Water Bottles and Comfortable Bedsocks
The Wonderful World Of Wheel-Balancing - by Ken U.R. Dull

Fiction
*The Wonderful War On Serbia - How It Saved Lives And Established A
    Lasting Peace In The Balkans*

63

INDEX